COPYRIGHT © 2020 ASHLEY WARMINGTON 2021

ALL RIGHTS RESERVED.

ISBN:9781795350396

DEDICATION

I DEDICATE THIS BOOK TO DEAN JOANN ROLLE. YOU ARE AN INSPIRATION TO EVERY ENTREPRENEUR. YOU HAVE TOUCHED THE LIVES OF US ALL. YOU ARE A CHANGE AGENT AND A FORCE OF NATURE. THE GODMOTHER OF ENTREPRENEURSHIP.THANK YOU FOR YOUR LOVE AND SUPPORT.

TABLE OF CONTENTS

ACKNOWLEDGMENTS

I WOULD LIKE TO ACKNOWLEDGE MY
MOTHER. SHE TAUGHT ME THE LIFE
LESSONS THAT I WILL USE TO THE VERY
END. THANK YOU MOM.

ABOUT THE AUTHOR

Ashley Warmington, MBA is the owner and founder of the New York's #1 Airbnb management company. Ms. Warmington went from homeless to becoming the Queen of Airbnb. She built a company from the principles of "Honest, Reliability, Consistency and a Positive Attitude." Ms. Warmington has learned the economic power behind your Airbnb is in your team, which starts with your cleaning specialist. This book shows you step by step on how to find the key element to your business. Ms. Warmington explains everything from writing the job description to critiquing their work.

 Ms. Warmington is also the founder of Warmington Cleaning Academy, where she trains and consults cleaning business owners. She currently resides in NYS and has expanded her business to Federal and city contracts.

PREFACE

Are you a business owner or an employee? One of the biggest mistakes business owners make is that they never devise a plan for delegating areas of the business. As an Airbnb business owner, it starts with your cleaning team. This guide is meant to prepare you for being the best in the business. This guide will give you an edge because you decided to become an expert in an area many business owners do not invest in; building a team. It is harder than fundraising or even finding clients. I have been through a plethora of obstacles to write this book.

You are the captain of your ship. Your mindset will determine who you let on your boat and where you end up. Airbnb can look like a quick buck but you will soon find out that it is an intricate business that demands you wear multiple hats. The cleaning crew you work with is just one aspect of the team but the most important. These individuals are not just scrubbing toilets and making beds in between guests. They are your eyes and ears. They are an extension of your principles and expectations. If you implement these tips, who are on the fast track to building your Airbnb empire.

INTRODUCTION
WHAT IS IT ALL ABOUT

Starting a short term rental means learning the art of accounting and delegation. If you master the finances and hire the right support staff yours will be a successful business. This is a guide to hiring and getting the best from your most important team member (aside from your lawyer and accountant); your cleaner. A cleaner is your stage manager, responsible for when the door opens, and when it closes and the guests depart, their professionalism is what they will remember, and review. At Cozy Oasis, we are professional cleaners. You'll get great reviews, repeat business and word of mouth referrals because we've learned a simple equation:

$$\frac{\text{Great Communication} + \text{A Clean Airbnb}}{\$\$\text{Great Review}\$\$}$$

We are committed to ensuring your guests have a worry-free experience and enjoy super clean lodging. It seems obvious and it actually is.

I started Cozy Oasis 5 years ago to provide a top-tier professional cleaning service specifically tailored for short-term rentals. I am committed to a level of cleanliness that hosts and guests would recognize and praise. It doesn't seem like a long time but the amount of mistakes and risks

I made added up to at least a lifetime. I followed Steve Jobs mantra "Fail fast". It allowed me to learn what were the cornerstones of the business and where I should put the most effort. The cornerstone of our business is our staff.

The cleaning industry has a 200% employee turnover rate. It took us the first 3 years to figure out to create the perfect job description, hiring process, orientation and quality control system. It all led us to develop a company culture of excellence and accountability.Our clients are relying on me to place several layers of offense in my hiring process. That is why I am writing this book. As an Airbnb entrepreneur, you need to know that the most common pitfalls will be in building your property maintenance team.

Candid Moment#1

In the early years of starting Cozy Oasis, I advertised on sites like craigslist looking for cleaners. My client list was growing exponentially and I needed to add people to the team. I, myself, was managing 7-9 locations. The first cleaners I had were college students. I had no idea I needed to train and monitor their work. I had what the cleaning industry calls "warm body syndrome" . I hired irregulars of experience, my job description was one paragraph and couldn't figure out the proper amount to pay them. I spent the first 2 years cleaning behind cleaners and fixing mistakes that could have been avoided from the job description. Follow along to avoid the mistakes I made.

SHOULD I HIRE A COMPANY OR AN INDEPENDENT PERSON?

The first question you want to ask yourself is how big is your operation. How many properties to have currently? Another question to ask yourself is, how many bookings to expect to have per month. Are you doing monthly stays or 3-4 nights? The answers to these questions will help you decide how many times a week/month you will need a cleaning service. Below are the pros and cons of both options

Pros of Hiring a Cleaning Company
- Last minute availability
- Will not disappear
- Can cover large operations
- Insurance, workman's compensation and bonding included in the price
- Accountability and management is outsourced
- They are a business as well and will respect your product

Cons of Hiring A Cleaning Company
- Higher pricing (to cover the cost of insurance, workman's compensation and bonding.)
- Different cleaners each cleaning.
- Less personalization in the requirements for cleaning

Pros of Hiring an Independent Cleaner

- Trainable on the preferences and nuances of your property
- Easily accessible when addressing issues or last minute requests
- Typically priced at a lower rate
- Can expand the job description with less bureaucracy

Cons of Hiring an Independent Cleaner

- Inflexible schedule
- No backup in case of vacations, emergencies or sickness
- Can quit at a moments notice
- No insurance

Do your research on the hiring laws in your city and state? You need to know the difference between a W9 and a W2 employee and how these two distinctions will effect your taxes.

WHERE CAN YOU FIND THE BEST?
THE SEARCH

Googling for a cleaning company will lead you down an infinite rabbit hole. To find the best company or individual you can speak to other hosts. In most cases, Airbnb owners give the job to their current housekeeper. If you do not have a connection to other hosts or a housekeeper, the next chapter will go into detail on advertising for the position.

In your county, city or town there are Airbnb hosts meetups. Attend to those to gain access to the list of cleaning companies and individuals who can help with your business. If you are not interested in attending meetings, there are also free Airbnb host Facebook groups. Ask someone if their cleaner needs more work or if there is a company they can recommend. Property managers are also members of the group, they will flood your inbox with proposals in and offers. In either case, you still need to read the next chapter. You need to know what to ask for and how to weed out companies and individuals who can't meet your needs.

Here are a few suggestions for where to search/advertise jobs for cleaning companies or independent cleaners:

- Classifieds
- Airbnb Facebook groups
- Local church or community center
- Friends and Family
- Airbnb meetups
- Local Workforce organizations

ADVERTISING FOR A CLEANING POSITION
EXPRESS YOURSELF

Be clear and detailed about your expectations

Describe how many bedrooms and bathrooms? Is it a duplex? Do you have a patio or balcony that needs maintenance?Will they manage the inventory of toiletries? Whether cleaning will be limited to guests leaving and setting up or cleaning will include several times while guests are in residence. Is laundry involved. Whether or not supplies will be provided?

Avoid

Never place unreasonable limits on how long they should be cleaning. The industry minimum is 2-3 hrs Be honest about how many times in the month you will need them. Choosing a professional cleaning specialist is like adding someone to your family or inner circle. They will have access to your property and are an integral part of your short term rental business. Have a definitive expectation of their duties and level of previous experience.

Compensation: By the Hr vs Flat Fee

Service positions have two types of payment arrangements. You can pay by the hour (the minimum should comply with your states laws.) if you have an in-depth understanding of your cash flow. Within this system, it is paramount that you create a budget that includes the maximum you are able to pay for cleanings. This limit is determined by your desired profit margin and the amount of time/costs it takes to clean your property.

If you are running your Airbnb like a business and not a charity you should know the maximum amount of time it takes to clean your property. Multiply that by average pay per hour in your state. Then have your set pay. The risk of using this system is when degenerate guests leave the property in a deplorable state. As a result, the cleaner has to stay longer, causing you to go over budget. A reputable service will notify you if extra hours are required before the cleaning starts.

* If the mess that is left behind by a guest is unreasonable, please make sure that the cleaner documents it BEFORE cleaning. Take the pictures and file a complaint with Airbnb so that you request additional funds from the guest to compensate for the deplorable conditions. A fee-based service is often more economical. It removes the time variable and permits us to assign our more versatile cleaners. You can pay on the high end of the spectrum, within reason, to ensure that the cleaner is being paid fairly for their time.

For business owners that are looking to expand their operations, a flat fee is the best way to manage costs. You can dictate a flat fee based on whether it is a studio, 1, 2, or 3+ bedroom. Be clear in the initial discussions about what you can expect to pay. Check the going rates. Discuss what are the service charges and what that includes. Services differ in what they offer. Compare. Remember the adage, in the end "you get what you pay for.," Cleaning is the major variable in guest reviews and repeat visits and recommendations. A sparkling rental pays dividends. Comb through your finances to assess what is your maximum.

Candid Moment#2

I once hired the perfect cleaner and lost her because the pay was not what she expected. I put the pay in the ad but 'forgot' to discuss it during the interview process. She completed her first cleaning and I sent her payment. It was safe to say she was not pleased. She had apparently applied to multiple jobs and did not remember what the pay was in the job description. I lost a good person because I was not clear on what

Require References

Ask for at least 2 references from cleaning-related jobs. Now matter how well the interview goes, you will need to verify their experience. Many cleaning specialists promise they can meet your turn-around schedules, but verify that they can do this. More experienced independent cleaners might have other private clients. Contact their clients to confirm if they truly have experience.

Job Description Template

TAKE A MOMENT WRITE

5 MUST HAVES FOR THE IDEAL CANDIDATE

_____

_____

_____

_____

_____

5 DEAL BREAKERS

_____

_____

_____

_____

_____

Write down how many bedrooms and bathrooms will they be responsible for cleaning? Location and proximity to public transportation Things that you require such as replacing supplies, inventory management, checking in guests? If so, what are these tasks and how will they be paid and/or reimbursed for these tasks?Will they be responsible for reporting damage, fixing broken pipes or toilets? Will you be available during the cleaning for questions or emergencies? Should they bring their own supplies?What is your check-in/out time scheduled? How many days in advance do you give them notice for cleanings?

Candid Moment#3

During the early years of Cozy Oasis, I spent months posting job descriptions at colleges and universities. Searching for that one or two college students who had a flexible schedule and some cleaning experience. I didn't get down to the nitty gritty of what I needed on my team.

Here are three actual job descriptions I posted on craigslist between 2015-2016:

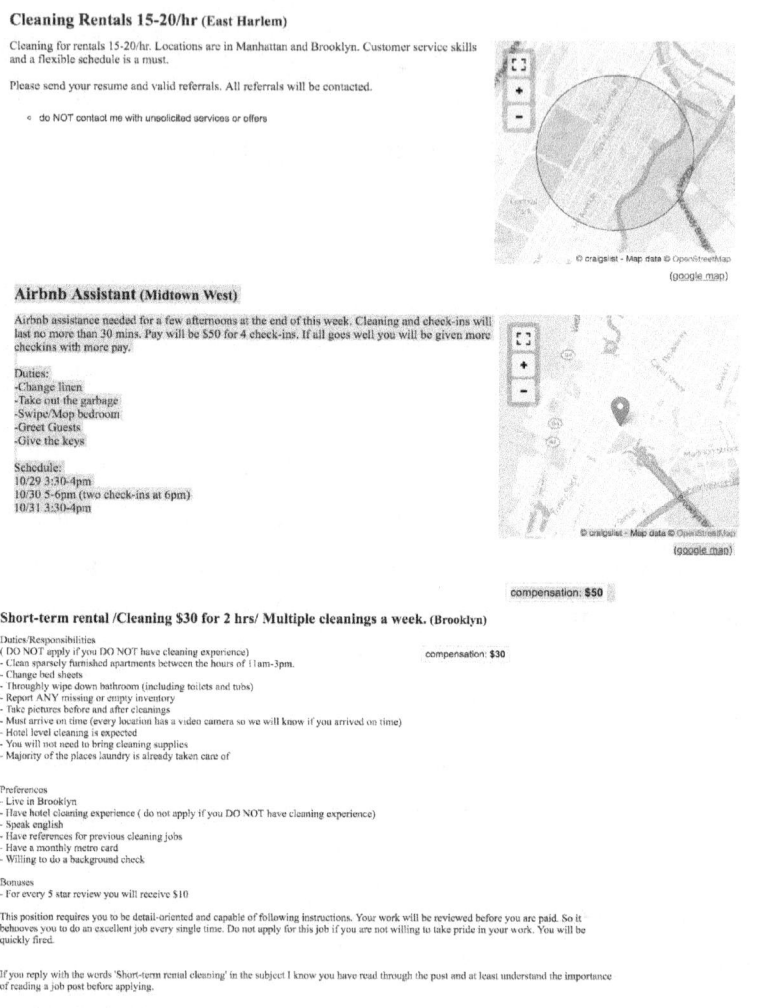

Cleaning Rentals 15-20/hr (East Harlem)

Cleaning for rentals 15-20/hr. Locations are in Manhattan and Brooklyn. Customer service skills and a flexible schedule is a must.

Please send your resume and valid referrals. All referrals will be contacted.

   « do NOT contact me with unsolicited services or offers

(google map)

Airbnb Assistant (Midtown West)

Airbnb assistance needed for a few afternoons at the end of this week. Cleaning and check-ins will last no more than 30 mins. Pay will be $50 for 4 check-ins. If all goes well you will be given more checkins with more pay.

Duties:
-Change linen
-Take out the garbage
-Swipe/Mop bedroom
-Greet Guests
-Give the keys

Schedule:
10/29 3:30-4pm
10/30 5-6pm (two check-ins at 6pm)
10/31 3:30-4pm

(google map)

compensation: $50

Short-term rental /Cleaning $30 for 2 hrs/ Multiple cleanings a week. (Brooklyn)

Duties/Responsibilities
(DO NOT apply if you DO NOT have cleaning experience)   compensation: $30
- Clean sparsely furnished apartments between the hours of 11am-3pm.
- Change bed sheets
- Throughly wipe down bathroom (including toilets and tubs)
- Report ANY missing or empty inventory
- Take pictures before and after cleanings
- Must arrive on time (every location has a video camera so we will know if you arrived on time)
- You will not need to bring cleaning supplies
- Majority of the places laundry is already taken care of

Preferences
- Live in Brooklyn
- Have hotel cleaning experience (do not apply if you DO NOT have cleaning experience)
- Speak english
- Have references for previous cleaning jobs
- Have a monthly metro card
- Willing to do a background check

Bonuses
- For every 5 star review you will receive $10

This position requires you to be detail-oriented and capable of following instructions. Your work will be reviewed before you are paid. So it behooves you to do an excellent job every single time. Do not apply for this job if you are not willing to take pride in your work. You will be quickly fired.

If you reply with the words 'Short-term rental cleaning' in the subject I know you have read through the post and at least understand the importance of reading a job post before applying.

As you can see, my job posts became more descriptive over time. It was because of all the mistakes I made in the hiring process. In these moments I realized that "common sense is not common". It was my job as the owner of my business to clearly state the expectations in the job description and then meticulously filter out individuals who were not a good fit.

INTERVIEWING PROCESS
THE ART OF THE PHONE INTERVIEW

The phone interview is the most convenient way to vet potential cleaning candidates. This is where you will quickly reject unqualified applicants and pool together the qualified candidates. Break the interview into three parts; first quiz them on the job post, second ask them why they applied and who they are, lastly let them know if you will be following up.

Job Post Quiz

You want to make sure that they are not just applying blindly to your post because you have keywords like 'cleaning'.

Ask them the following questions:
- What do you think of the posting?
- Have you done anything like this?
- If so, tell me?
- Tell me what you thought about the description and requirements for this position?Did anything in the post stand out to you?
- Tell me about your cleaning experience.
- What are some of your life goals?
- Why did you get into the cleaning industry?
- What is your availability like?Is the company insured?
- Who checks the lodging to be sure it was cleaned and how and when are these evaluations done?

*Any good candidate will have questions for you.

Why did they Apply?

You are not offering any health benefits, full-time work or an opportunity for upward mobility, so why are they applying to your job posting. You need to determine if they are going to take this position seriously, especially if you plan to have a hands-off approach.

Did I get the job?

End the conversation, letting them know that you will contact them in 48-72 hrs if they have a job. Continue searching for candidates until you are sure you are comfortable with meeting the candidate in-person and letting them onto your property.

PHONE INTERVIEW SCRIPT CHEAT SHEET

If interviewing candidates for a job is new for you, follow the script below to get you started:

Step 1
Call to schedule a phone interview. Give them a heads so they know to allocate a time, place and mindset for your conversation.

Step 2
Call on time, be ready with questions.

Interview Script:

Hi (cleaner's name), my name is (your name). We have a scheduled phone interview for the cleaning job at my short-term rental. Is now still a good time to talk?

Great! I wanted to get to know you before we get into the nitty gritty. Could you tell me what brought you into this field?

(Take time to listen and ask questions about what you hear. Then go into the following questions:)

How did you find the ad for this position? What about the ad specifically encouraged you to apply?
When were you looking to start? Do you foresee any barriers that may make the job difficult for you?

How do you typically receive payment for your services? Tell me your experience with cleaning short-term rentals. Which of the job requirements stood out to you?(

Once you feel you have a good idea of whether you want to work with this person, end the call on a good note.)

Thank you so much for taking the time to speak with me. I am sure you had a very busy day. I will look over my notes and if I think this is a good fit I will follow up with you in a few days.

Have a Good day!

ORIENTATION
HOW YOU PRACTICE IS HOW YOU PLAY

No two properties are exactly alike. At Cosy Oasis we send a team leader for the first visit, so we will know all the nuances of your property. This information is necessary for our team to be well prepared to service the space. We want you to show us your cleaning professional where everything is and how you would prefer your property to be presented to your guests. You must give your service provider an introduction to the systems you have put in place. Here are a few systems that should already be set:

Storage

Have a designated place for storing clean linen and cleaning supplies. Cosy Oasis cleaners bring their own basic supplies but if you prefer certain brands or methods, have them on hand. Always have a backup just in case. Show your Cleaning Specialist where everything is located. We're committed to having our specialists put back the supplies neatly after they've cleaned.

Laundry System

You should have set up a laundry system for linens prior to hiring your cleaning professional. At Cosy Oasis we will work with your local laundromat for pick up/drop off or be responsible for washing the laundry in house.

Checklists

Although we have our own check-list, write up a list of details for each room. For instance, let them know where you want to leave towels for the guests. How many pillows on each bed? How many rolls of toilet tissue should be left in the bathroom.

Damage Reporting and Solutions

We require our clients to provide an emergency call list and whether you prefer them to call, email, or text. If you are unattainable during various times of the day , we also prefer that you provide a call list of plumbers and handymen.

Suggestions

After meeting in your rental for the first time, at Cosy Oasis, we may make recommendations to augment your lists and ours. We are always willing to talk about additional costs and whether or not it adds value. This is your property and you are the decision-maker. Because we're in this business and have surveyed the competitive frame-work and recognize best practices, we can give you a perspective on what has been successful for others.. Remember, the relationship between you and your service provider is symbiotic. With an open dialogue, we can learn from each other. Our goal is to give you a rental unit that sparkles. An alliance between us will make that happen.

Candid Moment #4

One of my first hires was a college student. He showed up on time and cleaned the entire apartment in excellent timing. I was elated that I found a great addition to my company. But I noticed that the quilt was not on the bed. I asked him about it and he said it was in the dryer. The dread and anxiety washed over my entire body. The guests were going to arrive in 15 minutes. When I asked him to wash the duvet cover, I assumed he knew that a duvet cover was the linen that covered the duvet/quilt. It was my fault for not demonstrating how to remove the duvet cover. During an orientation, show the cleaning company or cleaner everything. Do not assume, like I did, that they already know.

SUPPLIES/EQUIPMENT

You want success, you must invest to assure that your Cleaning Specialist has the ability to complete all the necessary tasks. (However, legally a W9 independent contractor should not expect you to provide them with supplies.) Please discuss this with your accountant, especially if you are hiring an independent cleaner.

Below is a preliminary list of items the guests and the Cleaning Specialist will need:

Basic Supply List
Window/Mirror Cleaning
Bathroom and Shower and toilet cleaner
Rags and dusters
Dishwashing Liquid
Detergent Wood
Air FreshenerWD-40 (you would be surprised)
Sponges
Rags
Paper Towel

Recommended Basic Guest Supplies
Handsoap
Shampoo/Conditioner
Dishwashing liquid
Sponges
Toilet tissue, paper towels, napkins
Coffee/tea

On our introductory visit at Cosy Oasis our supervisor will do an inventory of your cleaning equipment and guest supplies.

The Importance of Providing your own Supplies of Equipment

Believe it or not it is cost effective. How? For one, you will avoid the cleaner not being able to complete a task because they forgot certain supplies or ran out during the cleaning. Thus leading to a bad experience for the guests. If you prefer certain products and want to ensure your furniture and fixtures are protected from the commercial substances used by most cleaning services, supply your own. It's also good to have everything on hand in case your guests need to clean up a toilet, a dirty sink, a spill..

Lastly, the supplies purchased for your short-term rental are tax deductible. Consult with your accountant about itemized deductions in accordance with your city and state laws to confirm these benefits.

GIVING CRITICISM
CLEAR CONVERSATIONS
BRING CLEAR
UNDERSTANDING

Clear Conversations Bring Clear Understanding is my family's mantra. My parents are very honest; sometimes too honest. However, their standards and expectations are always clear and understandable. This is because of two things. First setting the standards in the initial conversation and secondly having follow up conversations when the standards are not met. It has definitely prepared for being a business owner.

Setting the Standard

We started off with a job description because that is where you set the standard. You explain to the cleaning service or candidate what you are looking for while simultaneously deterring who will not meet your requirements from applying. Be honest about your pet peeves and your values. If you value things like communication, honesty and prior experience, put that in the job requirements.

Offer Guest Feedback (Good and Bad)

We like feedback from your guests. Cleaning Specialists who take pride in their work want to hear what they can do to improve or what they did great on. We learn from their experiences. Offering feedback from the guests can provide valuable criticism on their workmanship. It also stresses the correlation between your ability to pay them and guest reviews. Put it like an equation

Bad workmanship + Bad reviews = bad listing.

Summary :A bad listing is where no one wants to stay and therefore you will go out of business. The cleaner will lose money. Make sure to explain this to your cleaning specialist.

Do Your Own Surprise Checkup

We supervise and review our cleaners and we recommend that you do too.We recommend that you leave a debris marker; a toy under the sofa, a book behind the toilet, a dust-bunny under the bed. After the first cleaning check to see if it's there. After the first couple of cleanings, review your checklist with them. See if we need to add more to the list. Not everything is intuitive. After the initial cleaning, talk to your cleaner and review your concerns.

If you still think this is a good fit, give the Cleaning Specialist an appraise of what they did well, and what was missed. If the cleaning was way below your standards, release them to find their destiny. Cleaning may not be the field for them. When dealing with a professional cleaning company, like Cozy Oasis, they should dispatch another cleaner.

Candid Moment #5

I had to transition from thinking I was an annoying perfectionist to a leader with expectations. The design of the company was based on Jeff Bezos Day 1 mentality; it's always about the customer's needs. But I spent a lot of time taking care of mistakes because I didn't put in measures that enforced expectations. I hired a cleaner that made it very clear to me his expectation was to be paid $30/hr. He supposedly had years of experience. I showed up during the last 10 minutes of the scheduled cleaning. Surprise! It was nowhere near done. I did this 2 more times, changing the time I showed up. The second time I was waiting for him to arrive and start the cleaning. The last time I arrived shortly after he left. He was irritated that I was checking his work. But I caught so many mistakes that could have destroyed my company.

THE FOUR CORPORATE FRIENDLY LOVE LANGUAGES

When you find a great cleaning specialist, the next step is to keep them. Create incentives and reward systems, that are clearly outlined, so that you establish career-financial goals. The lack of upward mobility is a major reason talent leaves the company. It will be no different for your cleaner. For instance, every five star review in cleaning, the cleaner can get a flat fee bonus. This will keep your cleaning specialist on their toes and gives them financial-based motivation. However, money is not everyone's love language and therefore may not be a motivating factor. Below is a list of the Four Corporate-Friendly Love Languages, along with some suggestions on how to express gratitude towards your cleaner.

Words of affirmation
- Send text messages or emails stating "Good job" or "Wow, the place smelled amazing!"
- Send them screenshots of guest reviews that explicitly discuss their workmanship
- Write them a Thank You note

Gifts
- Gift cards every quarter (every 3 months)
- Give them their birthday off
- A $5 bonus every time a guest leaves a five star review for cleaning.

Acts of Service

- Send them in a cab ride to the train or home during bad weather
- Throw out the garbage
- Restock the supply closet

Quality time

- Take them out for coffee
- Chat with them before or after a cleaning
- Monthly phone conversations

MONITORING THEIR WORK
WHAT THE EYES DO NOT SEE, THE HEART WILL NOT MISS

This is probably the hardest part of hiring a cleaner. You must be diligent about supervising their work without causing yourself grief.

Surprise Checkups

As previously mentioned, even though we supervise and inspect, we like our hosts to check up on our cleaners unexpectedly. Especially in the first 90 days. If you are not able to, have a friend or family pop in.

Pay Once the Work is Finished

Again, this is about a service, and you can state your billing policyHave a setup where payment is predicated on the completion of the task. Once guests have confirmed that the place is clean then send payment. If issues are found, require that the cleaner returns to fix the issues. This only works if you have a good relationship with your cleaner and you have agreed on this system during the phone interview.This is a necessary tool to have whether you hire a Cleaning Specialist or not. You need

Creating Checklists

Create checklists that must be signed before the cleaner leaves the property. At Cozy Oasis we have an electronic checklist that requires photo evidence as well. If you notice the cleaners are signing off on items that were not completed, that is ground for a dismal. Lying is an easy way to get fired at Cozy Oasis.

LETTING YOUR CLEANING SPECIALIST GO
LET IT GO, LET IT FLOW

From time-to-time, we know hosts decide to change cleaning services. Or you may be ready to move from an individual cleaner to a service. Breakups can be difficult but it does not need to be painful. Not everyone can meet your standards, and that is okay. Don't feel bad and don't make the person who is on able to meet your standards feel bad. Sometimes it can feel like people are choosing not to meet your standards. But in my experience, people truly do their best. However, if their best is not enough it is time to release them to their destiny. Here are some tips on how to detaching yourself from your current cleaner or service without it disrupting your business:

Keep Records
The Clear Conversation Brings Clear Understanding reappears in this section. If you have been having honest conversations throughout their probation then they should not be surprised the conversation is happening. You should be able to pull up dates, pictures and guest comments that will assist you in letting them go.

Change Key Access
You will feel better about the conversation once you know they no longer have access to your property. Change the lockbox code and the locks if you have given them keys.

Have A Backup Cleaner

Before you let them go, ensure that your new service provider is ready and available to begin. This prevents you from having to keep an inefficient cleaner that causes you to have bad reviews.

CONCLUSION

Now you are ready to build your cleaning team. Entrepreneurship is only for the select few. Do not expect everyone to have the same motivations and drive as you. It is up to you to attract quality professionals and reciprocate their efforts. I wrote this book because you should not have to endure the same obstacles I did. By reading this book, your journey has been cut in half. Heed my warning when I say 'Hire Slow and Fire Fast'. It will be the pinnacle of your hiring journey. You don't want too many on your boat that can sink it and you don't want to keep people who have shown they will sink it.

I truly wish the best and I would be excited to hear your success story. If you want a consultation on your hiring process, reach out to us. Our number is 347-377-2496. We want to see you succeed.

www.ingramcontent.com/pod-product-compliance
Lightning Source LLC
Chambersburg PA
CBHW070931220526
45468CB00005B/1740